Guide Dog School

by Frances Morris

SCHOOL PUBLISHERS

Cover, ©Paul Doyle/Alamy; p.3, ©Jim Craigmyle/CORBIS; p.4, ©Gary Randall/Taxi/Getty Images; p.5, ©Phil Walter/Getty Images; p.6, ©Don Mason/Corbis; p.7, ©AP Photo/Casa Grande Dispatch, Steven King; p.8, ©Randy Faris/Corbis; p.9, ©Lynn Stone/Animals Animals; p.10, ©Frank Naylor/Alamy; p.11, ©Mark Richard/PhotoEdit; p.12, ©Jim Craigmyle/Corbis; p.13, ©PA/Topham/The Image Works; p.14, ©Zuma Press.

Printed in China

ISBN 10: 0-15-351441-8
ISBN 13: 978-0-15-351441-8

Ordering Options
ISBN 10: 0-15-351213-X (Grade 3 Advanced Collection)
ISBN 13: 978-0-15-351213-1 (Grade 3 Advanced Collection)
ISBN 10: 0-15-358076-3 (package of 5)
ISBN 13: 978-0-15-358076-5 (package of 5)

3 4 5 6 7 8 9 10 985 12 11 10 09 08

Taking the Lead

Lucky trots confidently down the street as Josh follows slightly behind. Josh holds the leash that is attached to Lucky's harness.

There is a branch lying on the sidewalk. Lucky carefully pulls Josh around it. Lucky won't let Josh move forward until he is certain the way is clear.

Lucky is a guide dog. He has been trained to help people who are blind. Guide dogs lead people through traffic. They let them know where there is a curb to step off. Guide dogs give freedom to people who are blind.

The path to becoming a guide dog begins almost at birth. Guide dog schools usually raise their own puppies. The staff at the school feeds them and takes care of them. They also watch carefully to find out if a puppy is friendly or scared of loud noises. Does the puppy like to learn?

The staff makes these important decisions early. A nervous or shy puppy might not make a good guide dog, but the puppy will make a fine pet. Many people are glad to adopt these puppies.

Puppy Kindergarten

The other puppies go to live with puppy raisers when they are three months old. Puppy raisers take the future guide dogs into their homes. This is an important time for the puppies. They get to know people. They discover the world. The time spent with the puppy raisers is like puppy kindergarten.

Puppy raisers are volunteers. Many are even children! Some puppy raisers belong to clubs, so they work with the puppies as a project. The club members help each other.

One puppy raiser takes care of the puppy. The person feeds the puppy, brushes the puppy's coat, and walks it. The puppy learns that this person cares for it. The puppy also learns to care for the person. This is very important because a guide dog must make many important decisions that help keep the person safe. The dog needs to want to help the person. A dog that is well cared for will feel this way.

Puppy raisers have many chores. They instruct the puppies to walk slightly ahead because guide dogs have to lead people. The dogs are not supposed to walk beside people.

The puppies also learn to come, lie down, and sit. Most importantly, the puppies go everywhere. The puppies go to stores, parks, towns, and even to visit other dogs. They ride in cars and on trains and buses because as guide dogs, they must be prepared for many different situations.

The puppies remain in the puppy raisers' homes for about a year. Then they return to guide dog school. Upon return, the school checks the puppies' health and then retests them. Again, some may not be right for the life of a guide dog. These puppies return to their raisers' homes or go to live with another volunteer family. The dogs that pass the tests have more skills to learn.

Learning to Guide

Each dog works with one trainer. This tutor teaches the dog about keeping a person safe. First, the dogs learn how to wear harnesses, which are the dogs' uniforms. They help the dogs to pull people who are blind gently in the right direction.

The dogs learn to recognize more commands. The dogs must know "forward," "stop," "right," and "left." The people who the dogs guide will give these important directions to the dogs.

Curbs are another important lesson. Many people who are blind count curbs to help find their way. The dogs must stop each time they see a curb.

Trainers will fall off a curb and pretend to be hurt. This gets the dogs' attention because they care about the trainers. Soon the dogs know to stop when they see a curb. Next they learn to sit at curbs where the people must step down. The dogs learn to put their paws on curbs where the people must step up.

Some things might not hurt dogs but could hurt people. A dog could walk under a tree branch hanging in the street. People who are blind, however, would walk into it, so dogs must learn to identify these dangers, too.

Sometimes people may put themselves in danger. A person may give a "forward" command at a street corner, but the dog sees an oncoming car. It has learned that cars are dangerous. It will not obey. This is called "intelligent disobedience." The dog understands that obeying the command will be dangerous.

Dogs may want to follow a smell or want to play with another dog. Guide dogs can't do this. "City days" help them learn how to behave in the city. They get used to sounds, smells, and heavy traffic. They learn about trains and buses. They practice climbing up the steps and learn to sit at their trainers' feet.

Guide dogs learn about the country, too. They learn to walk without sidewalks or curbs and to follow a line of grass along a road.

Ready to Go!

After training, the dogs take a test. The trainers wear a blindfold for the test. The dogs must rely on their own resources. If the dogs pass the test, they are matched with people who are blind.

The new owners then spend a month at the guide dog school where they learn how to give commands and how to care for their new dogs. By the end of the month, the dog and person have become a team.

Some schools have a special day where the puppy raisers meet the grown dogs and their new owners. It is a chance for the puppy raisers to see and be proud of their work. It also gives the new owners the chance to thank the puppy raisers.

Guide dogs are now part of our culture. They have a very important and serious job.

Think Critically

1. What do guide dogs do at curbs?

2. Which section would you read to find out about "city days"?

3. What is "intelligent disobedience"?

4. Why do you think the author wrote this book?

5. Would you want to be a puppy raiser? Why or why not?

 Social Studies

Write an Article Write an article about a guide dog puppy for the local newspaper. Make sure you include information that you learned from this story.

School-Home Connection Walk around your house. Look for places where a guide dog could help a person who is blind. Make a list of the places. Explain how the dog could help the person.

Word Count: 980

We Can Use Coins

by Tammy Jones

I need to know these words.

dime

nickel

penny

quarter

3

Look at the coins.

Can you name the coins?

5

What coin does this boy have?

This boy has a penny.

A penny is worth 1 cent.

6

7

What coin does this girl have?
This girl has a nickel.
A nickel is worth 5 cents.

8

9

Look at this boy.

What coin does he have?

He has a dime.

A dime is worth 10 cents.

11

Look at this girl.

What coin does she have?

She has a quarter.

A quarter is worth 25 cents.

13

You can use coins.
You can put coins in
a parking meter.

14

You can put coins in
a telephone.

15

What does this girl do with her coins?